URGENCY

Category: Business & Economics

Description: How to be more enthusiastic and get more done. This is one of 13 books based on Benjamin Franklin's 13-week self improvement program (Ben Franklin's 13 virtues) that will show you how to be more enthusiastic and get things done now. After reading this book and focusing on being more energetic for one week you will learn how to have a sense of urgency that is as fast as a bolt of lightening. When you receive an emergency call from a customer you will discover how to immediately respond with massive action and a whatever-it-takes approach to solve the problem.

Copyright Bob Oros-2017

ISBN 978-1-105-22691-5

Written and published by Bob Oros

405-751-9191 Email Bob@BobOros.com

Web site www.BobOros.com

URGENCY 1

Urgency Be enthusiastic get things done now 5

UPOD 5

Get jacked up 12

It boils down to this 17

Is it this simple 23

ATNA 25

Spectator or doer 30

Why motivation programs fail 34

Responsibility with a time limit 38

Street smart 40

Urgency: Be enthusiastic get things done now 48

My 4% improvement objective: 49

What the entire book series will do for you 50

Ben Franklin's system 51

Achieve a 52% improvement 57

About the author Bob Oros (BobOros.com), ... 59

Urgency
Be enthusiastic get things done now

UPOD

Our economy has proven ONE THING over and over again. The customer is KING. All those people who think that companies are in business to make something, produce something, deliver something, or fix something are finding out that if no one buys their products or services they are history. And in my mind, that is a good thing. When anyone in the company thinks that taking care of a customer is someone else's job, well, the handwriting is on the wall.

Our economy is a SALES DRIVEN ECONOMY, PERIOD. You and I, and every other person who spends a dollar on anything have proven that. If we don't get the customer service we expect, we are gone to a competitor in a New York minute. (For those of you who are reading this from New Zealand, Australia or Canada, a New York minute is 45 seconds!)

And since we are ALL selling something, it is more important that YOU keep the edge on YOUR own service that you provide. Your competitors are hungry and they are after YOUR business. And in some cases, they are successful in taking away a customer. I want to challenge you to do ONE thing today that will make a huge difference in how your business grows. I want you to commit to using the UPOD strategy.

Have you ever heard of the acronym UPOD? If not you are in for one of the most impressive selling strategies you will ever use.

But first, let me ask you a couple of questions. How you answer will help you examine yourself and see if you have the internal drive that will help you take full advantage of the UPOD strategy.

Are you hungry? Do you want more? To succeed in sales you MUST be hungry and have a strong desire for success.

The key question to ask yourself: "What motivates me to keep doing the things that are necessary for success?"

Am I a goal setter, do I have personal and financial goals big enough to make me do the things the failures do not like to do?

There are many sales people who are content to pick up the small orders without any desire for a bigger piece of the pie. You must be the type of sales person who looks for the opportunity to polish your skills every day. By giving your best performance on every call and always asking yourself how you could have done better - you can be classified as a true professional.

I am used to dealing with professionals. I can tell a professional before I even meet them in person. They have a single quality that shows up in everything they do. And when you deal with someone who is NOT a professional, you sure can tell the difference. Do you have this quality? Can you guess what it is?

Here is an example of what this single quality is NOT!

I am selling two of my properties. I am not using a real estate broker, simply because the folks who are buying the properties are currently living in them. I have contacted the mortgage broker to arrange for the financing, the closing company to handle the paperwork, and you would think the rest would be simple. All you need is 4 or 5 documents to go along with the application. Well, it is like pulling teeth to get those documents. All kinds of delays. Every excuse you can think of. I have spent more time chasing around to get things done than you can imagine. After three weeks it STILL isn't done. It should have taken one day at the most!

Now let me give you another example.

A client of mine called and wanted to set up a series of three seminars for their customers. Within 5 minutes Ray and I had all the details worked out. Within 24 hours Ray had the locations, the times, the initial promotional piece, lunch arrangements for our participants, and the announcement out to his sales team. THAT is what you call a "sense of urgency!" THAT is what you call being a professional. THAT is why they are a leading distributor in the Midwest. THAT IS THE SINGLE QUALITY.

As a professional you always have the feeling that there are things that need to be done. Not from pressure or stress, but because you WANT to get them done. They are on your TO DO list and are there for a reason. You are motivated by end results and keep your eyes on the big picture, the overall plan and objectives.

Do you call your customers when there is a potential problem? For example, if a product is short on their order do you call your customer in advance and let them know, or do you let it go by and hope they have enough left in stock to get them by?

When you hear a piece of news that could possibly affect one of your customer's do you make it a special point to let them know, or do you assume they will get the information themselves?

When one of your customers has a problem and calls you for help, do you drop everything and do "whatever it takes" to help with the solution, or do you hesitate and hope that by the time you return the call the problem will go away?

That is the true mark of a professional. That is the single quality: A sense of urgency!

A sense of urgency is a skill that can be developed with practice. By adopting an attitude of "do it now" you can solve many small problems before they turn in a lost sale or a lost customer. By taking care of things immediately you impress your customers more than you can imagine.

Small things like returning phone calls within minutes rather than hours, dropping thank you cards in the mail the same day rather than two or three days later (if at all), make a big difference.

Now for the UPOD. A while ago I used this with an editor I was working with. He was much more impressed with my use of the UPOD strategy than if I had done things the normal way. UPOD stands for Under Promise Over Deliver. I received an email and was asked if I had any more articles. I told him it would take a couple of days. I then kicked in the UPOD (I have used this so often it has become a habit). I sent him an article within ten minutes. Here's the editor's response "That was the fastest couple of days in history."

Try it the next time a customer calls and asks for something. Give them a longer period of time and then kick in your "sense of urgency," your "whatever it takes," your "desire for success" attitude, and watch the response you get!

Get jacked up

How about showing a little passion for what you do? There is just too much ho-hum selling going on today. There are too many sales people who just don't get the fact that enthusiasm is contagious and as a sales person you have to infect everyone with a good dose of excitement.

So how do you get jacked up?

Here's how to get UN-jacked. Tell yourself you are a loser. Tell yourself you hate what you do. Tell yourself you will never make the sale. Tell yourself your company sucks. Tell yourself you never got any of the breaks. Tell yourself the competition is ruthless. Tell yourself that everybody buys on price. Tell yourself that your sales territory is saturated and there is no business.

Do you know what ninety-five percent of everyone in prison were told over and over again as they were growing up: "You are going to end up in prison some day?" Think about it. Over and over again they were told they were going to end up in prison some day. What if they were told something different? What if they were told over and over again that they might be in a little trouble right now, but they will get past it? What if they were told that they were going to grow up and be successful? Would that make a difference? The stuff you put in your mind is what controls your actions. So to get jacked up you have to put things in your mind that will get you excited and passionate about what you do for a living.

Put this affirmation in your mind. Carry it around with you and watch the difference...

(READ THIS LIKE YOU MEAN IT!) I am excited! I stay focused on all the good things I have to be excited about. I am excited about my career, my opportunities and my challenges. My excitement drives me to do everything with energy and enthusiasm. My mind is focused fully on what I am doing and I am able to get things done by telling myself to "DO IT NOW". I am excited and act enthusiastic and everyone around me catches it. Every time I see someone I know or meet someone new I am excited and enthusiastic about seeing them. By being enthusiastic, excited and full of energy I am a more valuable person. Energy and enthusiasm guarantees my success as a highly paid professional sales person. Energy, passion and enthusiasm will attract customers and sales to me. This energy will be like a magnet and attract bigger customers and larger commissions to me. I am going to give everything I have to everything I do.

Don't be a daydreamer. Don't wish you were somewhere else doing something different. Life is what it is. For whatever reason, you are where you are right now so you have to deal with it. Keep this quote on your dashboard: "My job is not to see what lies dimly at a distance, but to do what lies clearly at hand!" That means there is no getting around it... you have to make the prospecting call, send the email, mail the letter, take care of the follow up and keep going.

Forget about whether you feel like it or not. Actions come before feelings. ACT enthusiastic and your feelings will follow. If you wait until you FEEL jacked up you will be like the woman sitting on the park bench who turned into a skeleton waiting for the perfect man. It isn't gonna happen!

Here is another way to stay excited about what you are doing. Make training a DAILY part of your schedule. Spend time EVERYDAY learning something new about your business. Get excited about bringing news and information to your customers. In other words, start selling like you mean business. There is no excuse not to! Don't think it is up to the company to train you. It is up to you. Take responsibility. Invest in yourself. Read a book, take a course, listen to a motivational CD, read your marketing product sheets.

So the bottom line. Learn something new today. Get your butt out there and make something happen. Call someone. Go visit a customer and bring them a new idea. Stop whining. No one said it was going to be easy! Your customers need help making good decisions. Go help them make the decision to buy from you by being excited, enthusiastic and jacked up! Let them know you really want their business!

It boils down to this

The reason you are a successful sales person or the reason you barely get by.

One thing!!!

It can make a difference in less than 60 seconds. This one thing can clear away all the confusion and unorganized thoughts that are holding you back from really making a difference. Not only in your selling career but just as important in your income, personal life and family life.

You can recognize this one thing in a person the moment you meet them. I can easily spot the ones who have this one thing when I am talking before a team of sales people.

What is it?

The one thing that makes a successful sales person is this: they have decided that they are going to be a success. They don't waste time every day re-deciding. Before they go to bed at night they picture themselves having a successful day tomorrow. At the end of each day they go over the sales calls they made today and examine them as if they were a scientist looking for clues about how they could do better.

In the current competitive market if you go to your customer's only half decided that you are going to really bring them value, you might as well call in sick. If you are only half decided and your competitor has made the decision that they are going to win, you might as well give up, because you are fighting an unfair battle. You are going into battle with no bullets in your rifle, while your competitor is locked and loaded.

By making this DECISION that you are going to apply yourself 100% to your current position everything else falls into place. When you make a firm decision to be the best you call into action unknown powers that help you stay motivated. When you make the decision to be the best you stir up the DESIRE to succeed.

Once you make the decision you AUTOMATICALLY know that you must become a MASTER at the seven selling skills. You know that you must be BRILLIANT at the basics.

Then, if you reinforce your DECISION for 21 days it will be imbedded in your mind.

I am going to share with you a secret. Many people don't want you to know this secret because it is so powerful. This secret has been used all through history by kings, presidents, religious leaders, big companies, TV shows, advertisers, politicians, parents, coaches and teachers. It is also used by gang leaders, drug pushers, criminals, bullies, thieves and even the friends you hang out with.

This secret has stood the test of time. In one form or another, this secret been used since the beginning of mankind. Many successful people have used this secret to reach their goals. Many people swear that the discovery of this secret is the single most important event in their lifetime.

Here's the secret...

Nearly every minute of the day you are being controlled. How? By the words and pictures you allow people to put in your mind.

The repetition of positive or negative words and pictures day after day begins to affect you, for good or for bad. And the computer in your mind begins to make you do the things that the words and pictures represent. The use of this secret is one of the oldest practices of civilization.

The Boy Scout Oath, the Girl Scout oath, the Pledge of Allegiance to the flag, the prayers you are taught and the marriage vows are all forms of putting positive words and images in your mind. These positive words make you do positive things.

Marketing companies who want you to buy things use words, pictures and TV commercials that make you want to buy things from them.

Politicians use words and pictures to make you want to vote for them.

Drug pushers use words and pictures to make people buy drugs and get high.

Whether you end up a great success in your sales career or you end up a loser living on the street, it will be because of THE IMAGES AND WORDS YOU USED TO PROGRAM YOUR MIND.

And it all comes back to the one thing. Have you made the decision to give it your best shot? To fill your mind with pictures and words that clearly identify your success?

Or are you letting CNN and Headline News determine you fate?

Is it this simple

A study conducted on the failure of sales people discovered an amazing fact.

Out of 2,347 sales people employed by leading concerns in twenty-seven lines of business during a one year period, 1,482 of them failed before the year ended.

The fact that 63 per cent of the total number failed means that nearly two sales people failed for every one who was successful.

The reasons for this high rate of failure? 97% Lack of industry 37% Discouragement 12% Failure to follow instructions 8% Lack of product knowledge 4% Dishonesty 2% Poor health.

Think about it! 97% of the people who failed simply didn't do the work! And the work is making calls.

Show me a person of average ability who diligently gets out of the door early every morning, makes contact with 10 to 15 customers or potential customers every day and I will show you a person who is destined to succeed.

If you worked as hard on selling as warehouse employees, delivery drivers or meat cutters work at their jobs, your sales would double.

Don't get me wrong. There are plenty of us who know how to put in a good days work. You are most likely one of them. There are plenty of top sales people who know that they paid a price for all the business they have. I know several sales people who are in the five to ten million dollar a year arena. Ask any of them how they are able to sell so much and they will tell you the same thing. They work their tail off! They are hungry and ambitious.

How did we get so soft? When did we start thinking that it wasn't necessary to call on more customers? I think it started when someone came up with what they thought was a satisfactory number of customers or prospects to call on. There is no satisfactory number. You have to call on however many it takes to move x number of cases out of the warehouse or to sell x number of products. I know a sales rep in Las Vegas who has 6 accounts and sells thirty million dollars a year! I know another rep in Alabama who has 80 accounts and sells six million a year.

ATNA

You know the type. They tell you about all the big plans they have, all the great things they are going to do and end up doing nothing! Being an ATNA is kind of like buying on credit. They get the "high" of showing off what they bought, but they don't pay their bill.

How can you make the next 12 months the best year you have ever had? How can you exceed your goals and sales plan in spite of the slow down in the economy. In spite of the bleak news you hear every night on the TV? In spite of the fact that growth for many companies has to come from a competitor because there is no "new" business?

If you want to have a fantastic year here's what you have to do:

You have to stop setting goals that are out of your control.

Let me explain.

You want to open up 10 new accounts or add 10 new customers in the next 90 days. Sounds like a pretty good goal. However, it sounds like a goal someone infected with ATNA would make. How do you know if you can open 10 new accounts in 90 days? You don't! But you can make it sound good. You can jump up in the sales meeting and shout "I CAN DO IT - I CAN OPEN 10 NEW ACCOUNTS IN 90 DAYS!" And my response to that kind of rhetoric is "sit down and zip it up! You are a professional sales person, not an employee of some fly-by-night company who requires their sales staff to jump up and down, hollering and screaming to get psyched up before hitting the street!"

So, how do you set a meaningful goal? The goal has to be focused on the activities. Let's say you are calling on 30 accounts per week. If you set a goal to add 10 new meaningful prospects and call on them every week for 90 days, bring them ideas, ask them meaningful questions, and most importantly, FOLLOW UP on what you say, you can accomplish your goal. You can match your progress to the precise steps necessary to accomplish the goal. Because your goal is based on activities that you have in your power to do.

However, it doesn't sound as glamorous when you jump up in the sales meeting and say "I CAN ADD 10 NEW, HIGHLY QUALIFIED, WORTHWHILE PROSPECTS TO MY WEEKLY CALL ACTIVITIES AND GIVE THEM ALL THE ATTENTION, SERVICE AND FOLLOW UP THEY ARE NOT GETTING FROM THEIR CURRENT VENDOR!"

If you really want to make it a fantastic year you have to cure yourself of the ATNA syndrome and focus on the ACTION AND FOLLOW UP.

I recently attended a real estate seminar and the speaker told a great story about the topic of setting goals. He returned home from Viet Nam and was told that due to the injury in his leg he would always walk with a limp and never be able to run.

Here is what he did. He set a goal to SHOW UP at the track every morning at 6:00 AM dressed and ready to run. He didn't set a goal to RUN, only to SHOW UP READY TO RUN. Showing up was under his direct control. He discovered that since he was already at the track and dressed to run HE MIGHT AS WELL GIVE IT A TRY.

I don't need to tell you how the story ended. Because you just don't show up at the track dressed to run and NOT TAKE A FEW STEPS. And then, as you continue to show up, a few more steps, and a few more steps, until you are RUNNING.

It is the same thing with selling. It is impossible to SHOW UP at the prospect's business and BE READY TO SELL WITHOUT AT LEAST TAKING A FEW STEPS.

Spectator or doer

Over the years I have bought and sold several rental properties. One of my recent houses needed some yard work done. The back yard sloped towards the house and caused a water problem. I was going to build a deck but first I needed to work on solving the water problem.

I started with a shovel. That lasted about 15 minutes. I knew there had to be a better way so I headed to the equipment rental company.

After I arrived and looked over the options, I decided on a Bobcat. A Bobcat is a small tractor with a bucket on the front that scoops up the dirt. The person renting me the equipment asked if I knew how to operate it. I said "of course" thinking to myself "how hard can it be?" I hooked it up to my truck and headed home.

I pulled up behind my house, sat in the bobcat seat and prepared to pull it off the trailer. I started the engine, let out the clutch and lost control. It jerked ahead and by the time I figured how to stop it I had run into the gas meter and caused a gas leak. I immediately called the gas company and they were there in a matter of minutes to fix it.

I got back on the Bobcat and as I was turning around I lost control again and destroyed two sections of my fence.

As soon as I started digging my wife opened the door and said the TV cable was out. I told her to call the cable company and she said the phone didn't work. The only thing I didn't damage was the water main.

Twice during the day my neighbor, who is about 85 years old, walked over, looked at what I was doing, shook his head and walked away. At this point I really didn't need any criticism.

At the end of the day – after 8 hours - my yard sloped the right way. I was putting the Bobcat back on the trailer when my neighbor came over. I was expecting him to tell me I was crazy. Instead he said something that turned out to be the best compliment I have ever received. He said there are two kinds of people in the world. There are "spectators" and there are "doers." And then he walked away.

I have been selling my whole life and I know hundreds of selling techniques. But there is only one thing that will make you any money in the selling profession: you have to take action.

In a recent study about why CEO's fail (based on researching about 30 CEO's who had failed in the last 10 years) one of the most interesting things discovered was that once a failed CEO resigned, many of the organizations quickly rebounded under a new CEO. It would seem the CEO was the difference. However, the study came to a fairly simple conclusion. CEO's don't fail due to lack of strategy or a grand vision. They fail in execution: They simply don't take action.

The same is true of sales professionals and their account relationships. A colleague of mine was recently doing interviews for a client to determine why some customers switched to the competition and others hadn't. Many of the sales people who lost the accounts made reference to problems with the product, delivery, service, etc. My colleague's investigation showed the only common denominator was not the problems, but whether or not the sales person took action to solve the problems.

In the battle of sales we can take the advice of General Douglas Macarthur. Here is what he had to say on the subject: "The history of failure in war can be summed up in two words: too late. Too late in comprehending the deadly purpose of a potential enemy; too late in realizing the mortal danger; too late in preparedness; too late in uniting all possible forces for resistance; too late in standing with one's friends."

Are you a spectator or a doer? Someone who watches or takes action?

Why motivation programs fail

Do you have a good education? Do you know more about your products than anybody? Have you read every book you can find on selling? Do you listen to motivational CDs while driving? Do you read all the trade journals? Do you attend seminars and take pages of notes? Do you ask successful sales people for advice?

If you do - IT DOESN'T MATTER! That's right!

You may be fooling yourself and maybe some of your colleagues into thinking you are really going places. But it doesn't really matter. I am going to tell you to do something that is going to shock your system.

>Take all your motivational CDs and burn them!

>Take your library of selling books to the dump!

>Take your list of big impressive goals and tear it up!

Why would I give you that kind of advice? Because I am trying to help you. I want you to be more successful. You see, in sales, none of those things really make much difference. Here is what I mean.

Read this next paragraph carefully.

...You can have a great amount of knowledge
...read all types of positive thinking books
...listen to motivation and self help CDs
...write down big impressive goals and plans
...and be no farther ahead than a year ago
...unless you apply what you know!
UNLESS YOU APPLY WHAT YOU KNOW!

I am not saying that it is not a great accomplishment to have a degree or it is not important to listen to motivation CDs. I mean that many folks fail in sales because they don't apply what they learn. They never use the information to for their personal motivation. They don't take action. They don't have a sense of urgency!

Once you start to DO the things necessary for success you will find that you have what it takes. You will never know where you need to improve until you put yourself in front of the buyer and let him or her tell you the reasons they are not going to buy. You will then have experience. You will then have specific information to work on. You will then be able to put together a plan of attack based on actual feedback.

Take it from someone who does all those things. And it doesn't make me an additional dime. Unless I take one specific skill or strategy at a time and APPLY IT!

Knowledge is not the answer.

The answer to personal motivation is...

APPLICATION of specific knowledge.

APPLICATION OF THE PRINCIPLES OF SELLING.

If you read something that you remember reading in the past, ask yourself this: Did I apply it - or did I just read it?

Responsibility with a time limit

I was once in a sales meeting where the VP of Sales addressed a sales team of over 400 and said: "Our sales increase objective is 15%! 10% is not an option, 14% is not an option! It's 15% or you walk."

If you are having to tell people that they need to produce 15% or they are out the door then you're losing the race before you even start. You should have a system and that system should be the method of your success. But that's another topic.

I know that seems harsh, however, looking at it from management's point of view, they have expenses and require a certain level of sales to keep the payroll met, the lights turned on and the benefits active. As one sales manager put it: "Do you want to be the one to tell the customer service rep that the sale wasn't made in time so we are not going to pay you your full wage this week and your kids are not going be able to buy their school supplies."

A commissioned sales person shares this feeling of pressure; a salaried sales person does not share this feeling of pressure immediately however, they will eventually feel it. A commissioned sales person makes a certain number of sales each week or the mortgage doesn't get paid. The mortgage company will not say "no problem, we will catch you next month." We are really all commissioned sales people whether we are receiving a salary or a direct commission. A salary is based on the anticipation that a certain number of sales will be made in a timely matter, no matter what your position in the company.

Again, sales is not a luxury, but a responsibility with a time limit for expected results...

In the business section of today's news paper there is a headline that reads "Applebee's to close 24 low-earning restaurants."

The article goes on to say "Applebee's International Inc. said it will close 24 restaurants that aren't meeting performance goals."

In other words they are not making their sales numbers fast enough to keep up with their expenses. An additional thought on this might be what makes someone a leader.

Street smart

It was getting dark and the traffic was heavy. I pulled off the highway to take a look at my map to be sure I didn't pass the exit I was looking for. I was heading west on interstate 20 just west of Atlanta. As soon as I pulled into a MacDonald's I learned the real meaning of being "street smart." A young man about 28 years old approached my car with a bottle of Windex in his hand. He said he needed money and he was willing to work for it. He wanted to wash my windows.

I travel a lot and I am approached by many homeless people, however, this guy seemed a little different. He had a sincere look on his face along with a slight smile that immediately removed any feelings of worry that he might be dangerous. I asked him what his name was and he said Chad.

I told Chad it wasn't necessary to wash my windows and I bluntly asked him why an obviously talented guy like him was living on the street. He said he got out of jail three weeks ago and can't find a job. He said the standard answer everyone gives him is come back after the first of the year. He said he has been to every place within walking distance with no luck.

I asked Chad if he had a driver's license. He said he did but couldn't get a copy of it. He said it's a catch 22. You can't get a drivers license without a birth certificate and you can't get a birth certificate without identification. I asked him where he was staying and how long it has been since he had something to eat. He sleeps during the day and tries to get enough money in the evening to get by for the day. He said he hadn't eaten yet.

I invited him in to MacDonald's where we ordered dinner and sat down to eat. Chad seemed friendly and willing to talk, so I asked him some question to see if I might help point him in the right direction.

Do you have a family? "A wife and two kids, but they won't have anything to do with me.

Why were you in jail? He said he would rather not tell me. I pushed and asked him again. He said he didn't want me to be tempted to try it. I told him he didn't have to worry - I wasn't into anything illegal. He said he found a way to take the ink off of 5 dollar bills and turn them into 50's. He said everything was going good until he got caught and got sent to jail for 18 months.

Where are your from? Chad was originally from Indiana but ran away from home when he was twelve years old. He started selling drugs and by the time he was 18 he had his own home paid for and was doing really well. Then he got caught and sent to jail. After he got out it was one thing after another until he came across the counterfeiting idea. That lasted a few years until he got caught again. He said he didn't have an education and could never get a job that paid more that minimum wage.

What's going to be your next scam? This was the question I was leading up to. I studied his answer carefully to see if I could sense whether he was telling the truth. He said, very sincerely, there are no more scams. If someone walked up and offered him the surest thing that could not fail, he would turn it down.

How many people help you out? He said about 2 in 10. Out of the 10, some of them are downright mean and tell me to beat it or get lost, some of them just ignore me, and some of them threaten to call the police. But I just keep going looking for that one in five. Every now and then you find someone who goes out of their way to be helpful. A lady pulled up last week and gave me two turkey dinners. I took them to some friends of mine who were on the street and not able to get money as well as I could and gave the dinners to them. On the down side, I walked up to the drive up window to buy a sandwich because the dining room was closed, and the girl called the police.

You said you didn't have an education, but you sure got a lot of "street smarts." Chad asked me what I meant, so

I asked him to tell me everything he knew about me. He said I was from out of town because my license plate said Florida, but that's not were you are from because there was a rental tag on the dashboard, so you probably flew in from somewhere. You do some kind of work with people because you were not afraid to talk to me like a lot of folks. You have 9 one dollar bills in your wallet and about 4 twenty dollar bills. You probably have a family and are successful at what you do.

I told Chad that is what you call genuine street smarts. I asked him how he developed the skill.

"Being in jail and living on the street you learn these things automatically. You have to be totally aware of everything that is going on around you every minute of the day. You might be in danger and have to take off, or you might miss an opportunity if you are not paying

attention. After a while it becomes a habit and it's impossible NOT to do it."

And there is our answer to what it means to be street smart. Apply that to your everyday sales and watch your business take off!!

For the next hour I gave Chad all the help and guidance I could. I encouraged him to look for a job in direct sales. Any sales manager who would not give this guy a chance would have to have his or her head examined. Chad had more raw sales talent then anyone I have ever met.

As I was leaving I gave Chad enough money to last a few days, buy a new set of clothes and told him to go to the truck stop, get cleaned up and head to the employment office.

Will Chad take my advice? Was I scammed? It doesn't matter. Chad taught me a great lesson.

Urgency: Be enthusiastic get things done now

I have a sense of urgency that is as fast as a bolt of lightening. When I receive an emergency call from a customer I immediately respond with massive action and a whatever-it-takes approach to solve the problem. I return phone calls immediately. My reaction time is measured in minutes not hours or days. If I see a problem coming I call my customer in advance and begin solving the problem before it even begins. My highest priority is serving my customer and I take full responsibility for my actions and the actions of my company. My customer knows they can count on me and they never worry because I am their insurance policy against frustration and unresolved problems.

My 4% improvement objective:

_____

_____

_____

_____

_____

_____

What the entire book series will do for you

Buying all 13 books is like buying a library of 13 powerful coaching sessions that will increase every skill necessary for generating business. Once you experience the seemingly effortless improvement you will understand why there is a picture of Ben Franklin on every 100 dollar bill.

You will learn how to improve relationships, improve management skills, be more productive, generate more customers, negotiate better contracts, open new accounts, earn more profits and create more sales! Results most people only dream about! If you are a sales professional or an entrepreneur this is the perfect program to boost your sales and increase your profits.

Ben Franklin's system

In our fast paced business and personal life today it has become increasingly difficult to set aside time for self development and improving your skills. With every spare minute taken up by reading blogs, logging on to Facebook, following people on Twitter, responding to text messages and emails and constantly talking on your cell phone, there seems to be little, if any, time left for learning new skills. Even the quiet time behind the wheel of your car is no longer available with satellite radio and cell phone coverage in every corner of the country.

Even though this seems like a new problem, distractions have been around forever. Two hundred years ago a man by the name of Ben Franklin had the same problem.

He concluded that it was not a matter of distractions as much as a matter of focus. He set out to solve the problem and created the most effective system for self improvement ever invented.

Ben Franklin gives credit for all his success and accomplishments to the implementation of this system for the success he sought after. Despite being born into a poor family and only receiving two years of formal schooling, Ben Franklin became a successful printer, scientist, musician, author and one of the founding fathers of the United States. Ben Franklin is considered to have been one of the most persuasive and successful people in the history of the United States. He was a very skilled sales person, marketer, negotiator and copywriter. Skills that every business owner, professional person, manager and marketer should have.

In the year 1723, Ben Franklin, at the age of seventeen, arrived in Philadelphia without a penny to his name. At age 42, he retired, wealthy, the first self made millionaire in the country. Few people, before or since have ever been as successful as Benjamin Franklin. He gave credit for his many inventions and business successes to his system for self improvement he created when he was 20 years old.

The key to Franklin's success was his drive to constantly improve himself and accomplish his ambitions. In order to accomplish his goal, Franklin developed and committed himself to a personal improvement program that consisted of mastering 13 principles.

When he was seventy-nine years old, Benjamin Franklin wrote more about this idea than anything else that ever happened to him in his entire life. He felt that he owed all his success and happiness to this one thing. Franklin wrote: "I hope, therefore, that some of my descendants may follow the example and reap the benefit."

Since success is developed by performing small and seemingly insignificant acts, you can use this method by reading and putting into practice the 13 skills that will guarantee your success in sales with scientific certainty.

This program takes advantage of Franklin's system and applies it to improving your skills as a sales professional. This program will show you how to dominate your market by first dominating yourself. By focusing on the 13 skills that make up a highly effective and successful sales professional. As these skills are improved your results and sales increases will also show a dramatic improvement.

The goal of going through the program the first time is to increase each skill by only four percent. With the accomplishment of this small improvement in each skill or attitude your overall improvement will be 52%. Those are results most people only dream about. However, you can accomplish this by investing as little as 45 minutes once a week reading one book and then focusing on improving the single skill during the rest of the week. The second week by reading the second book and focusing on that single skill during the week and so on until all 13 weeks are completed.

You can write the single word on the back of your business card and tape it to your dash board as a reminder. You can put this one word on your smart phone as a reminder as well as on your email signature, your Facebook page or you can even have something worthwhile to tweet about. One word, one week, one skill, one "I am" statement, 4% improvement objective and your subconscious mind will receive the message through all the clutter and act on it.

After the first time through the process you can do as Ben Franklin suggests and go through the program a second, third and fourth time. Get your whole sales team on the same page at the same time and you will experience a whirlwind of new excitement and new business. Or get a like minded colleague and join forces with accountability and focus.

Achieve a 52% improvement

Using Franklin's scientific program for learning your objective is to improve 4% in each area over 13 weeks.

1. Attitude Define what you want and go after it.
2. Respect Earn respect-no more comfort zone.
3. Service Help customers build their business.
4. Urgency Be enthusiastic get things done now.
5. Confidence Remove restrictions and limitations.
6. Persistence Keep going and never give up.
7. Planning Get big results by setting big goals.
8. Questions Ask questions that make the sale.
9. Attention Get attention with irresistible offers.
10. Presenting Give reasons why they should buy.
11. Objections Remove every roadblock to the sale.

12. Closing Ask for the order and get paid.
13. Follow up Remove all hope for competitors.

About the author Bob Oros (BobOros.com),

Bob Oros has been a full time speaker and author since 1992 with over 2,000 speaking engagements in all 50 states and several international locations as well as the author of 21 books on sales. Prior to starting his speaking career, Bob served six years in the US Navy as a Communications Specialist and then worked his way from a street sales person to the position of National Sales Manager for a Fortune 200 company.

CSP Award: Bob was awarded the designation of Certified Speaking Professional (CSP) by the National Speakers Association and the International Federation for Professional Speakers. Fewer than 10% of all speakers worldwide qualify for this award.

PWA Member: Bob is a member of the Professional Writers Alliance.

www.ingramcontent.com/pod-product-compliance
Lightning Source LLC
Chambersburg PA
CBHW072244170526

45158CB00002BA/1002